MW01240668

HOW CAN I
BE SURE?

How You Can Be Sure of Your Salvation

F. Wayne Mac Leod

Light To My Path Book Distribution

CONTENTS

PREFACE

This is a topical study on the subject of the assurance of salvation. As you begin, please be aware that the first two chapters may be difficult to read. I believe, however, that it is important for us to begin with an understanding that there are many things we cling to that are not in themselves a basis for assurance.

Personally, I believe we can have an assurance of forgiveness and a guarantee of eternal life. This assurance, however, is not based on anything we have done or will do but rather in what the Lord Jesus has done and is doing in us.

It is my hope that this simple study will help us see Christ and His work in a new way. I can only pray that it will help some to come to know Him for the first time. For others, I pray that it will bring a deeper confidence in His work on their behalf. May the Lord use this simple work to meet you wherever you are in your relationship with Him. - F. Wayne Mac Leod

1 - EASY SALVATION

Bernard de Perrot in his book "Les Plus Belles Pages de Finney" says that while only thirty percent of the great evangelist D.L Moody's converts remained firm, eighty-five percent of Charles Finney's converts persevered to their death. (De Perrot, Bernard, "Les Plus Belles Pages de Finney", Flavion-Florennes: Editions le Phare, 1979, page 123)

There is great debate over these statistics and it is not our purpose here to compare these two great evangelists. These figures, however, are disturbing. If de Perrot is right, this would indicate that up to 70% of those who make a profession of faith in Christ will not persevere to the end. If we bring this matter down to our own day, many of us know individuals who, at one time in life, made a profession of faith in Christ and then fell back into their former lifestyle. What is happening? Why are we seeing such staggering statistics?

I was in a meeting some time ago, where the speaker led her listeners in a short sinners' prayer. When the prayer was over she assured them that they were now God's children and guaranteed a place in heaven. For many people, becoming a Christian is as simple as going forward at an evangelistic meeting or praying a sinners' prayer. Please do not get me wrong. For some, salvation is just that simple. We cannot afford to assume, however, that everyone who does so in now a child of God.

In the age in which we live I can send money across the world in a matter of minutes. I can communicate with the entire world from the comfort of my computer. I send documents and pictures to destinations thousands of kilometres away through the internet without leaving my chair. Never in the history of the world have things been so easy and convenient. Has this been spilling over into our faith? Are we looking for a Christianity that is easy and convenient?

The message of the gospel is incredibly simple. The Bible tells in John 3:16 that:

God so loved the world that he gave his one and only Son, that whoever believes in him shall not perish but have eternal life.

This is the simple gospel. There is nothing complicated

about it. The person who believes on the Son has eternal life. God has not made it difficult. He has made the gospel so simple that even a child can grasp its significance and know the salvation of the Lord. While we believe in a simple gospel, we need to beware of an easy salvation. In our age of convenience and ease we have sometimes made salvation so easy that we equate it with the simple act of raising a hand or walking an aisle. There are those whose assurance of salvation is based solely on these external actions. The assurance of my salvation, however, must be based on something much more profound. Could it be that the reason Christianity is in the condition it is in today is because we have exchanged true salvation for a cheap and easy imitation?

The great preacher Jonathan Edwards challenged his congregation and readers to carefully examine their lives to be sure that the salvation they claimed to have experienced was indeed the real thing and not a cheap imitation:

> *Those who entertain the opinion and hope of themselves, that they are godly, should take great care to see that their foundation be right. Those that are in doubt should not give themselves rest till the matter be resolved.*

It is said of Jonathan Edwards that when someone came to him seeking assurance of salvation he would first challenge them to seek whether they were saved at all. Could it be that we are giving false assurance of salvation to those who are not believers at all? Could we, like the false prophets of Jeremiah's day, be proclaiming "peace, peace when there is no peace" (Jeremiah. 6:14)?

Any study on the question of the assurance of salvation should begin with a careful examination of ourselves to see if we truly know the salvation of the Lord. I trust that this brief study will enable you to come to grips with this all important question.

For Consideration:

Have you ever met an individual who made a profession of salvation but did not demonstrate this by a changed life?

How would you summarize the simple message of the gospel?

Is it possible that we do not have assurance of salvation because we have never truly been saved from our sins?

What is the difference between the simple gospel and an easy but false salvation? Is it possible to give a false hope to the unbeliever?

For Prayer:

Thank the Lord for the simplicity of the gospel message.

Ask God to show you whether the salvation you profess is real.

Ask God to give you grace to persevere in your walk with Him, demonstrating the truth of your salvation.

2 - FALSE HOPE

Some time ago I asked myself the question: How close can an individual get to being a Christian without actually being one? As I studied the teaching of Scripture I was astonished to see what they taught. Let me share with you some of these findings.

You Can Believe In God And Not Know The Salvation Of The Lord

There are many passages in Scripture which speak to this point. Listen to what James 2:19 tells us:

> *You believe that there is one God. Good! Even the demons believe that--and shudder.*

There is no one who understands that there is a God better than Satan and his demons. They, however, are far from Him. Their eternal destiny is sealed. We will not see them in heaven with those who belong to the Lord. You can believe in God like Satan and his demons and be separated eternally from Him.

Paul told the Romans in Romans 1:18-20 that belief in God is one of the most natural things in the world:

> *The wrath of God is being revealed from heaven against all the godlessness and wickedness of men who suppress the truth by their wickedness, since what may be known about God is plain to them, because God has made it plain to them. For since the creation of the world God's invisible qualities--his eternal power and divine nature--have been clearly seen, being understood from what has been made, so that men are without excuse.*

Creation testifies to the greatness of God. We see His gentle and loving care in the sun and the rain. We see His awesome power in the earthquake and the storm. We see His faithfulness in each breath we take or in each beat of our heart. The Psalmist tells us that it is only the fool who claims there is no God (see Psalm 14:1).

Paul continues in Romans 1.21 to say:

> *For although they knew God, they neither glorified him as God nor gave thanks to him, but their thinking became futile and their foolish hearts were darkened.*

Paul describes here a people who knew God but who were still in darkness. From this we understand that believing there is a God is not sufficient. Like the individuals Paul described here you can know about God and still be under His judgment.

You Can Live A Good Life And Not Be A True Believer

Let's move now from a belief in God to lifestyle. We have all met individuals who say they believe in God but whose life does not honour Him. Jesus often condemned the hypocrites of His day reminding them that a true belief in God ought to change our way of life.

Having said this, however, Scripture also teaches that it is possible to have both a belief in God and a good life and still not be a true believer. There are different examples of this in the Bible.

The first example is in Luke 18. In His travels, Jesus met a rich ruler. This ruler came to Jesus with a desire to know how he could inherit eternal life. From the context we understand that this man not only believed in God but also obeyed the commandments of Moses (see Luke 18:20-21). After speaking with this ruler, however, Jesus turned to His disciples in Luke 18:24-25 and said:

How hard it is for the rich to enter the kingdom of

God! Indeed, it is easier for a camel to go through the eye of a needle than for a rich man to enter the kingdom of God.

Here was a man who not only believed in God but also did his best to obey His commandments but according to Jesus He was not going to enter the kingdom of God.

In Acts 10 we read the story of Cornelius. Listen to how the Bible describes this man and his family in Acts 10:1-2:

At Caesarea there was a man named Cornelius, a centurion in what was known as the Italian Regiment. He and all his family were devout and God-fearing; he gave generously to those in need and prayed to God regularly.

There can be no doubt about the character of this man and his family. They believed in God and served Him with all their heart. Despite their belief in God and good life, one day an angel appeared to Cornelius. Listen to what this angel told him in Acts 11:13-14:

Send to Joppa for Simon who is called Peter. He will bring you a message through which you and all your household will be saved.

This verse shows us clearly that although Cornelius was

devout and God-fearing, he still needed to be saved. His beliefs and good works would not get him to heaven.

In John 3 we read about a Pharisee named Nicodemus. This man had many good qualities. As a Pharisee he not only believed in God but served Him religiously. There was no group in Israel as religious as the Pharisees. Listen, however, to what Jesus tells this God fearing religious man in John 3:3:

> In reply Jesus declared, "I tell you the truth, no one can see the kingdom of God unless he is born again."

The insinuation here is that Nicodemus, as good and as religious as he was, at this point in his life, was not going to see the kingdom of God. His good works and beliefs were not enough to make him a child of God.

All of these examples make it very clear that it is quite possible to believe in God and life a good life and still not be a true Christian.

You Can Have Great Sincerity And Zeal For The Lord And Not Be Saved

Let's add to the above qualities a zeal for the Lord and His work. The Bible tells us that it is possible to be very zealous for the Lord and His work and not be saved. We have already seen an example of this in the life of Cornelius. Let us reconsider this illustration.

Acts 10:1-2 tells us clearly that Cornelius was a devout and God fearing man. There can be no questioning his sincerity. This is clear in what the angel told him about his prayers and gifts in Acts 10:4:

> Cornelius stared at him in fear." What is it, Lord?" he asked. The angel answered, "Your prayers and gifts to the poor have come up as a memorial offering before God."

What do we understand from this verse? We understand that the prayers and service of Cornelius were acceptable to God. For them to be acceptable to God they had to have been offered from a heart that was sincere. Cornelius had a sincere heart in serving God. His heart was sincere but he was still invited to contact Peter so he and his family could be saved and become children of God.

The apostle Paul, told his readers in Romans 10:1-3 that even though the people of Israel were very sincere and zealous for God they were not saved:

> Brothers, my heart's desire and prayer to God for the Israelites is that they may be saved. For I can testify about them that they are zealous for God, but their zeal is not based on knowledge. Since they did not know the righteousness that comes from God and sought to establish their own, they did not submit to God's righteousness.

Israel's belief in God, her good works and her zeal for God were not enough. Despite all these good qualities Paul's prayer for them was that they be saved. Sincerity of heart and zeal for God are not sufficient to get you to heaven.

You Can Claim Him As "Lord" And Not Be In A Right Relationship

The Israelites of the Old Testament claimed that the Lord God was their God. Listen to what God said about them in Hosea 8:2:

> Israel cries out to me, "O our God, we acknowledge you!"

Israel acknowledged the Lord God as their God. The implication was that they recognized His lordship over their lives. We saw how Paul spoke about their religious zeal in this matter in Romans 10:1-3. The context of this passage indicates, however, that despite their claim, Israel was under God's judgment.

> But Israel has rejected what is good; an enemy will pursue him. (Hosea 8:3)

Listen to what the Lord Jesus said in Matthew 7:21:

*Not everyone who says to me, "Lord, Lord," will enter
the kingdom of heaven, but only he who does the will
of my Father who is in heaven.*

Many who claim Jesus as their Lord will not enter the
kingdom of heaven. I am convinced that some of these
people truly believe that they have given Him first place.
Some of them are sincerely trying to do His will and live
for Him.

Salvation goes far deeper than simply claiming Jesus is
God and following His teaching with sincerity. As Jesus
said, there will be many who call Him Lord who will not
enter the kingdom of heaven.

You Can Be Healed Through The Power Of Jesus' Name And Not Be A True Believer

When I was serving as a missionary on the island
of Reunion, I was in charge of a series of Bible
correspondence courses. In one of the lessons the
question was asked: "How do you know you are saved?"
One student responded by saying: "Several years ago
I was very sick. I prayed and God healed me. Now I
know I am saved." Here was an individual who had
experienced the touch of God in her life. God had healed
her. She was of the opinion, however, that because God
had touched her physically, she must be saved. There
could be nothing further from the truth. The New

Testament is filled with encounters between Jesus and the sick. Many individuals were healed by the power of the Lord Jesus but very few of them actually came to experience the salvation of God. The vast majority of those who were healed by Jesus rejected Him at His crucifixion.

Luke 17 tells us the story of ten lepers who came to Jesus for healing. Jesus told them to go their way. As they left His presence, they were all healed (Luke 11:14). Only one out of the ten, however, was sufficiently moved in his heart to return to the Lord Jesus to give Him praise and thanks. Even in this case, however, we are not told if this individual truly trusted the Lord Jesus for His eternal salvation. What this passage tells us is that we can be physically or emotionally touched by the Lord and still be lost in our sin.

You Can Be Delivered From The Powers Of Darkness Through Christ And Not Be Saved

Scripture also indicates that we can be delivered from evil spirits and still not enter into a saving relationship with the Lord Jesus. In Matthew 12:43-45, Jesus instructed His disciples about spiritual warfare. Listen to what He told them in this passage:

When an evil spirit comes out of a man, it goes through arid places seeking rest and does not find it. Then it says, "I will return to the house I left." When it arrives, it finds the house unoccupied, swept clean and put in order. Then it goes and takes with it seven other spirits more wicked than itself, and they go in and live there. And the final condition of that man is worse than the first. That is how it will be with this wicked generation.

In this scenario, Jesus told His disciples that it was possible for a person to be delivered of an evil spirit and, because He was still not in a right relationship with God, have that evil spirit return with others, making his final condition worse than the first. Notice particularly that the demon returns to find the house clean but "unoccupied." "Unoccupied" indicates that there was no demon present but neither was the presence of God!

While the Lord ministered on earth, He delivered many individuals from their evil spirits. No doubt, many of these individuals went on to live normal lives. Their normal lives, however, were still lives without Christ and without His salvation. God often touches the lives of unbelievers. In His grace He sees fit to heal them of their diseases and deliver them of their demons. Their deliverance however, is not a guarantee of salvation.

You Can Come To A Knowledge Of Who Christ Is And Not Be Saved From Your Sin

Romans 14:11 tells us that the day is coming when every knee will bow before the Lord Jesus and confess

Him as Lord. Even the enemies of Christ will one day come to acknowledge the person of the Lord Jesus and confess that He is Lord and Saviour. This recognition, however, will follow them into an eternal separation from God and His salvation.

It is clear in Scripture that even the demons of hell have a full awareness of the person of the Lord Jesus. This is quite clear from Luke 4.41:

> *Moreover, demons came out of many people, shouting, 'You are the Son of God!' But he rebuked them and would not allow them to speak, because they knew he was the Christ."*

There was no question in the minds of these demons as to the person of the Lord Jesus. They knew He was the Christ, the anointed one of God come to save His people from sin. That knowledge, however, was not sufficient to give these demons a place in heaven. Like these demons, there are many who believe Jesus Christ is the Son of God come to save us from our sins. A recognition of His person and work is not sufficient to save these demons. It takes more than a simple recognition of who Jesus is and what He came to do to become a child of God.

You Can Tremble Because Of Your Sins And Not Be Saved

The Bible tells us that it is possible for us to tremble because of our sin and still not be a true believer. James 2:19 tells us:

You believe that there is one God. Good! Even the demons believe that--and shudder."

While we have already examined this passage under another heading it merits another look. The verse tells us that the demons believe in God and shudder. Why do these demons shudder? They shudder because of who God is and the reality of their judgment. They know their end is coming. They know they will be judged for their sin. They know that their eternity will be an eternity of torment and suffering. For all their trembling, however, they are not saved.

In Revelation 6:15-17 we are told that on the day of judgment those who are not the children of God will call out for the mountains and the rocks to fall on them and hide them from the wrath of the Lamb of God. They do so because they are fully aware of the wrath that is to come. They know what their future holds. They know that they do not belong to the Lord Jesus and will spend eternity without Him. They tremble at the thought but they are not saved.

The fact of the matter is this. An unbeliever can be sorry for his or her sin. They may turn their back on certain sins and never return to them again. Turning from past sins and changing our lives may make us better people but it does not make us Christians.

An unbeliever may have a clear understanding of his or her destiny without Christ, and even tremble at the thought of life under His judgment. For all their fear and trembling, however, they are not saved. I have spoken to people who tell me clearly that they know they are going to hell. Some of them fear this reality but they have never come to Christ to accept His salvation.

You Can Earnestly Desire The Word Of God And Not Be A True Christian

We often attribute a desire for the Word of God with salvation. Listen however to what Luke 8:13 tells us:

Those on the rock are the ones who receive the word with joy when they hear it, but they have no root. They believe for a while, but in the time of testing they fall away.

In the parable of the sower, Jesus told His listeners that the seed that fell on the stony soil was like those who received the Word with joy when they heard it but because they had no root they fell away. This verse is significant. It tells us that it is possible for an unbeliever to be excited about the truth of the Word and enjoy hearing it proclaimed but still never experience the salvation of the Lord.

The writer of Hebrews speaks about this in Hebrews 6:4-6 when he says:

> *It is impossible for those who have once been enlightened, who have tasted the heavenly gift, who have shared in the Holy Spirit, who have tasted the goodness of the word of God and the powers of the coming age, if they fall away, to be brought back to repentance, because to their loss they are crucifying the Son of God all over again and subjecting him to public disgrace."*

This is a difficult passage to understand. What is clear from this, however, is that it is possible to have *tasted the goodness of the Word of God and still perish in sin*. The commentator Matthew Henry interprets this passage it this way:

> *They may have some relish of gospel doctrines, may hear the word with pleasure, may remember much of it, and talk well of it, and yet never be cast into the form and mould of it nor have it dwelling richly in them. (Henry, Matthew, Matthew Henry's Commentary, New Jersey: Fleming H. Revell Company, Volume VI, page 913)*

These individuals know and love the truth but have very little evidence of any personal relationship with God.

You Can Experience The Empowering Of The Holy Spirit And Not Be Saved

It is clear from the teaching of the New Testament that an individual may have an experience with the Holy Spirit and even be empowered by Him to do a particular task and yet never be a child of God. In Hebrews 6.4 we read that it was possible for an individual to share in the Holy Spirit and fall away never to be restored.

Jesus tells us clearly in Matthew 7:22-23 that in the last days there will be those who prophesy, cast out demons, and do miracles in His name that will be turned away from heaven.

> *Many will say to me on that day, "Lord, Lord, did we not prophesy in your name, and in your name drive out demons and perform many miracles?" Then I will tell them plainly, "I never knew you. Away from me, you evildoers!"*

God, in His sovereignty, can use even an unbeliever to advance His kingdom. Though these individuals are able to do great things in the name of Jesus they do not truly belong to Him. God can empower whomever He wishes to accomplish His purpose. In Scriptures we read how the Lord sent a great fish to swallow Jonah and spit Him up on dry land. He used a donkey to speak to Baalam. God is not limited to use only true believers.

You can be used of the Holy Spirit and not be a child of God.

What do we learn from all of these verses? We learn that we cannot base the assurance of our salvation on externals alone. While the true believer should bear fruit that shows he or she belongs to Christ, the assurance of our salvation is not based exclusively outward signs, actions or beliefs. Being a Christian in much more than doing good things, believing true doctrine and experiencing the touch of God on our lives. All these things are wonderful but not a sure enough sign that we belong to the Lord Jesus as His child.

I admit that this may be a difficult chapter for many to read. I remember sharing these truths in a church service some years ago and a man met me at the door of the church quite upset saying: "Hearing that message, nobody could ever be sure that they were saved."

I am sure that many who read this will have a similar reaction. The reality of the matter, however, is that it would do us all a lot of good to examine the basis for our assurance of salvation. Is it not better to question our salvation than to live with a false assurance? As we come to the end of this chapter we need to ask: Is our salvation real? Are we sure we are going to heaven? How can we know for sure? In the course of the next few chapters we will examine how we can be sure that the salvation we profess in genuine.

For Consideration:

While the true believer has a life that is changed by God are these external changes in themselves a guarantee of salvation?

Is it possible to believe or even preach all the right doctrines of the faith and yet still not belong to the Lord Jesus?

Can the Holy Spirit use those who do not belong to Him to accomplish His purpose?

How is it to be deceived by religious beliefs and practices into believing that a person is a true believer?

For Prayer:

Ask the Lord to help you not to be deceived into thinking that the measure of whether a person belongs to Him is good works and beliefs.

Ask the Lord to open the heart of those who have been basing their assurance on externals alone.

3 - CHRIST IN YOU

We saw in the last chapter that determining whether a person is truly a child of God is not a simple matter of looking at the externals. This leaves us now with a very important question: What is the difference between the believer and the unbeliever? What guarantees and gives me full assurance of salvation?

The apostle Paul addressed this question in Colossians 1:35-37. Listen to what he said about the good news of the gospel of Christ:

> *I have become its servant by the commission God gave me to present to you the word of God in its fullness-- the mystery that has been kept hidden for ages and generations, but is now disclosed to the saints. To them God has chosen to make known among the Gentiles the glorious riches of this mystery, which is Christ in you, the hope of glory.*

Paul told the Colossians in this passage that there was a mystery that had been hidden for generations. "This mystery," said Paul "is now being made known to the saints." He went on to tell the Colossians that this mystery was the message of "Christ in you the hope of glory."

We cannot miss the point Paul is making here. Jesus Christ in you is the hope of glory. Do you need assurance of future glory in the presence of God? According to the apostle Paul the secret of this hope is "Christ in you."

Let's go back to the original question we asked at the beginning of this chapter. What is the difference between the believer and the unbeliever? The difference is not always found in lifestyle or beliefs. We have all met good living people who are not Christians and Christians who are not always good living people. We have also met unbelievers who know a lot about the doctrines of Christianity and young believers who understand very little.

The one clear distinguishing feature between a believer and an unbeliever is Christ. I'm not speaking about knowledge about Christ here but about Christ Himself. As Paul said, it is "Christ in you" that makes the difference. Christ in you is your hope. The Spirit of Christ dwells in the life of the believer. The apostle Paul emphasizes this point in Romans 8:9 when he said:

You, however, are not in the flesh but in the Spirit, if

in fact the Spirit of God dwells in you. Anyone who does not have the Spirit of Christ does not belong to Him. (ESV)

Notice again what Paul is saying. He tells us that if a person does not have the Spirit of Christ in them they do not belong to God. Once again, the distinction between a believer and an unbeliever is Christ and His Spirit.

Speaking to the Colossians Paul said:

For you have died, and your life is hidden with Christ in God. When Christ who is your life appears, then you also will appear with him in glory. (Colossians 3:3-4, ESV)

Notice the phrase "... Christ who is your life." Where does our spiritual life come from? Our life is Christ. He is the source of our new life. It is His presence in us that is our life. This is far more than a human decision to change one's lifestyle. It is the very presence of Christ living in us and changing us from the inside.

Moses understood this way back in the Old Testament when he said to God in Exodus 33:15-16:

Then Moses said to him, "If your Presence does not go with us, do not send us up from here. How will anyone know that you are pleased with me and with your people unless you go with us? What else will

distinguish me and your people from all the other
people on the face of the earth?"

Do you see what Moses is saying here? He is telling
his readers that the one thing that distinguishes the
believer from the unbeliever is the presence of God. It
is not what I believe or what I do that makes me a
Christian, though these things are important—it is the
presence of the Lord God and His Spirit in my life.

The apostle Paul knew he had nothing to boast about in
himself. Writing in Philippians 3:3 he said:

For we are the circumcision, who worship by the Spirit
of God and glory in Christ Jesus and put no confidence
in the flesh.

From this we understand that, when it came to his
salvation Paul placed no confidence in the works of his
flesh. His hope of glory was in the person and presence
of the Lord Jesus alone. Writing in 2 Corinthians 10:17
he said: "But, 'Let him who boasts boast in the Lord.'"
Christ alone is our only boast. Nothing else will count.
God distinguishes His people from the rest of humanity
purely on the basis of the presence and work of Christ
in the life of the individual. Christ in us alone is our
guarantee of eternal life. He alone is our hope of ever
being able to stand before God. The apostle Paul put it
this way when he wrote in Philippians 3:8-9:

I consider everything a loss compared to the surpassing greatness of knowing Christ Jesus my Lord, for whose sake I have lost all things. I consider them rubbish, that I may gain Christ and be found in him, not having a righteousness of my own that comes from the law, but that which is through faith in Christ—the righteousness that comes from God and is by faith.

When the great apostle Paul stood before God on that final judgment day he knew that God would not guarantee him entrance into the kingdom of heaven because of his suffering for the cause of Christ or because of the great work he did to expand His kingdom. Despite all his efforts, Paul's only hope of eternal glory was the person of Christ and His presence and righteousness in him. Paul did not trust in himself, his efforts or his beliefs to get to heaven. His confidence was in the person of Christ, His work and His presence in His life.

In John 6:51 Jesus said:

I am the living bread that came down from heaven. If anyone eats of this bread, he will live forever. This bread is my flesh, which I will give for the life of the world."

The teaching of this passage is that if you want to have

eternal life you must eat the Bread of Life. Jesus is the Bread of Life. What does it mean to eat the Bread of Life? When we eat something we take it into ourselves and it becomes part of us. This is what the Lord Jesus is saying. If you want to have eternal life, you must open your heart to receive the person of Christ and His Spirit. He must come to live in you and become part of your life. Again it is important that we distinguish between believing things about Jesus and Jesus Himself. The Bread of Life here is not teaching about Jesus but Jesus Himself. If you want to "live forever" you need more than teaching, you need the person of Jesus.

1 John 5:12 makes this even clearer when the apostle writes:

> He who has the Son has life; he who does not have the Son of God does not have life.

This passage is very clear. If you have the Son of God in you, you have His life. If Jesus is not in you, you will perish.

All of these passages tell us that the hope of eternal life cannot be found in anything I do. It can only be found in one person alone. Jesus Christ in us alone is our guarantee of heaven.

This leads us to another important question. If our assurance of salvation is found in the person of Christ in us, how can we know if Christ is in us? What is the proof of His presence in my life?

If the person of Christ is in you, there will be evidence of this in your life. His life and His mind will become more and more evident. You will no longer be the same person. 2 Corinthians 5.17 says this about the believer:

Therefore, if anyone is in Christ, he is a new creation; the old has gone, the new has come!

Do you see what Paul is saying here? If we are in Christ (or if Christ is in us), then we will be different. The old things we used to enjoy, our old ways and thought patterns will begin to disappear.

While believers are not yet completely delivered from their old nature, the character of Christ begins to evidence itself in their lives. His love in them will be seen in their relationships with others. His humility and patience will begin to make itself known in the way they deal with family and friends. His forgiveness will be poured out on those who have offended them. They become aware of a new power in their lives. There is peace to overcome the trials that come their way that does not come from themselves. Their heart experiences joy as it never experienced before. That heart is broken by things that break God's heart. They are moved to worship as the Holy Spirit draws them to praise and thanksgiving. The sins they used to enjoy, they now find repulsive. There is a new excitement for the Word of God and the ways of God. They experience something that is not natural to their old nature. Christ's life is making itself evident in them.

It is important that we understand that we are speaking here about something that is happening in the believer not something he or she is doing in their own efforts. The love believers experience for those they once hated is not something they have trained themselves to do. It is Christ's love in them. The patience and joy they experience in their trials is completely foreign to their natural selves and often surprises them. There is a world of difference between those things we strive to attain in human strength and wisdom and the character of Christ being revealed in us. The one is human, the other is divine. The one shows us that even sinful man can do good things. The other shows that Christ is living and revealing Himself in us. There will be evidence of Christ's presence and the presence of His Spirit in the believer. When the Lord Jesus comes into a life, things will not be the same. How can they be the same, for the very presence of God's Holy Spirit is moving and shaping that life into the image of Christ?

What we need to see from this chapter is that the only real assurance we can ultimately have of our salvation is the person and work of Christ. It is not just a doctrine understood in our minds, but the actual person and work of the Lord Jesus in your heart today. It is only Christ in us who is our hope of eternal glory. If we want assurance of our salvation we must first look for the person and work of Christ in our lives. As the apostle

John says in 1 John 5:12:

> He who has the Son has life; he who does not have the
> Son of God does not have life.

Our assurance of salvation comes in the form of the
person and work of the Lord Jesus. He has done
everything necessary for our salvation. If we want to be
assured, we must take our eyes off ourselves and look to
what He has done and is doing in us today. We dare not
look to anything but Christ and his life in us if we are to
have any hope and confidence of future glory. His work
and His personal presence in my life is my only hope. He
alone is my guarantee. I cling to His presence in me and
His work on my behalf as my assurance.

For Consideration:

What is the difference between believing things about
Christ and the presence of Christ in us?

What is the difference between trying to do good things
for God and the Spirit of God doing good things in us
and through us?

Is there evidence of the presence of Christ and His Spirit
in you?

How does the truth of "Christ in us" move all the focus from us to Christ as our guarantee of salvation?

Could we ever have true assurance apart from Christ in us? Explain.

For Prayer:

Take a moment to thank the Lord Jesus that He comes to give us spiritual life and that His life in us is a guarantee of eternal salvation.

Take a moment today to ask the Lord to forgive you and to come to live in your heart.

Take a moment to thank the Lord Jesus that He willingly laid down His life to pay for the penalty of our sins and open the door for His Spirit to dwell in our heart guaranteeing our salvation.

4 - THE TESTIMONY OF HIS SPIRIT

We saw in the last chapter that the presence of Christ in us gives assurance of salvation. We know we are His because He lives in us and makes His presence known in our lives. If we want to be assured of salvation we need to seek evidence of Christ's presence in our lives.

As we continue in this study we also need to hear what the apostle Paul says in Romans 8:15-16:

> *For you did not receive a spirit that makes you a slave again to fear, but you received the Spirit of sonship. And by him we cry, "Abba, Father." The Spirit himself testifies with our spirit that we are God's children.*

Paul is telling us here that the real presence of the Spirit of Christ in us, communicates with our spirit reassuring us that we are God's children.

When Christ dwells in our heart, He does so in a very personal way. Listen to what Christ said to the church in Laodicea in Revelation 3:20:

> *Here I am! I stand at the door and knock. If anyone hears my voice and opens the door, I will come in and eat with him, and he with me."*

The picture here is of Christ wanting to come into the church of Laodicea. He told the believers that when they opened the door and allowed Him to come in, He would eat with them and they with Him. The Greek word used here for "eat" refers either to the principle meal of the day or to a feast. This is the type of meal you eat with your family and friends. This is the type of meal you eat where there is joy and festivity. There is intimacy, friendship and communion in this verse.

Notice that Christ promised not only that He would eat (fellowship) with His people but they would also eat or fellowship with Him. This cannot go unnoticed. We know that the heart of Christ is for fellowship with His people. Here, however, in this verse He tells us that the hearts of His people would also be moved to fellowship with Him. They too would delight in His presence and together they would commune as friend with friend.

Jesus describes for us in John 15:13-15 the type of relationship that He had with those who belong to him:

Greater love has no one than this that he lay down his life for his friends. You are my friends if you do what I command. I no longer call you servants, because a servant does not know his master's business. Instead, I have called you friends, for everything that I learned from my Father I have made known to you."

It is true that the Lord Jesus is our God. We owe Him everything. When He comes to live in our lives, however, He does so not only as God but also as our friend. There is an incredible intimacy in what the Lord tells us here. His presence is not an impersonal force in our lives but a deep friendship where there is intimacy and communion. He comforts us, reassures us and protects us as His friend.

James 1:5 tells us that when we need wisdom and guidance all we have to do is ask the Lord:

If any of you lacks wisdom, he should ask God, who gives generously to all without finding fault, and it will be given to him.

Philippians 4:13 tells us that when we don't have the strength to carry on, the power and enabling of this great Friend is at our disposal: "I can do everything through him who gives me strength."

This relationship with Christ is so personal that not only can we speak with Him but He also speaks with us and gives us the ability to hear His voice. "My sheep hear my voice, and I know them, and they follow me" (John 10:27, KJV). This voice, though not audible, is nonetheless very real and comforting. Who among us has not heard that inaudible voice leading, comforting or reassuring them in the pains and confusion of life?

As His children the Lord Jesus gives us ears to hear His voice. "Then Jesus said, 'He who has ears to hear, let him hear'" (Mark 4:9). The unbeliever may have a difficult time understanding this truth. For the believer, however, we know that voice of God in our spirit. We sense His directing and comforting presence and hear His Spirit speak to our Spirit. What an amazing thing it is to know these words of comfort and reassurance in our spirit.

It is for this reason that Spirit of Christ can testify "with our spirit that we are God's children" (Romans 8:16). As husbands and wives, we know how important it is to be reassured of the love and affection of our spouse. Even as friends, our relationship needs to be reaffirmed from time to time. God knows this human need and reassures us of His relationship by communicating with our spirit. He whispers: "You are mine" into our spiritual ears. He reassures us of our relationship with Him and of His presence in our lives.

This reassurance of the Spirit is very personal. Charles Spurgeon, in a sermon entitled "Full Assurance" said this:

Nothing short of a divine testimony in the soul will ever content the true Christian. The Spirit of God must Himself after a supernatural sort speak to our conscience and to our heart or else peaceful and quiet our spirit can never be. (Spurgeon, C.H., "Full Assurance" found at   http://www.spurgeon.org/ sermons/0384.html)

Those who truly belong to Christ hear this inner voice and are assured in their heart. Their spirit has been reassured by the Spirit of Christ. They have an inner peace and conviction that comes from the Spirit of God who intimately testifies to their spirit that they are loved and accepted by their God.

Listen to what Jesus said in John 8:42-44:

Jesus said to them, 'If God were your Father, you would love me, for I came from God and now am here. . . Why is my language not clear to you? Because you are unable to hear what I say. You belong to your father, the devil, and you want to carry out your father's desire. . .'

Notice that the Lord Jesus told the unbelievers of His

day that they could not hear Him because they did not belong to Him. To those who belong to Him, however, the Lord has given ears to hear His reassuring voice. His Spirit communicates with our spirit.

Do you want to know if you are truly His? You can know this by listening to the testimony of His Spirit to your heart. This voice is not to be confused with our own ideas and desires. It is the voice of a personal Friend and God who delights in reassuring us of our position in Him. It is a voice we can hear only because we have been given ears to hear.

Jesus knows our frail human nature. He knows how much we struggle with doubt. As a loving husband and friend, He wants us to be secure in our relationship with Him. It is His delight to remind us of His love and compassion for us. He does so by communicating this by means of the Holy Spirit to our heart, soul and mind. This assurance the Lord gives is far more than a feeling or a hope. It is a deep heartfelt conviction. It leads His children to say: "I know I am His." If you are His, you will hear His Spirit testifying to your spirit that you belong to Him.

What husband would want his wife to be unsure of His love and devotion to her? What parent would not grieve at the thought that their child never knew their love? God too has a deep desire to communicate His love and assurance to you personally. He will burn that assurance into your mind and heart. He will make it His commitment to reassure you lest you fail to understand

His desire for you. His Spirit will testify to your spirit and show you that you belong to Him.

If we want to have assurance of salvation, we need first to look for evidence of the presence and work of Christ in our lives. Second, we need to heed the reassuring testimony of the Spirit of God in our lives. The Spirit of God comes to give you assurance that you are a child of God. Those who belong to God know this inner convicting testimony of the Spirit of God. If you want to have assurance of your salvation you will need to listen to His inner voice of reassurance. This ultimately is very personal matter between you and your God. The true believer, however, is one who has been reassured in his or her heart by the Spirit of God.

For Consideration:

How does the personal presence of God's Spirit communicate with the believer?

Why is it important that the believer hear specifically from God in this matter of assurance of salvation? Is there any other voice that can bring such assurance?

Has the Spirit of God been speaking to your spirit how has His voice reassured you?

For Prayer:

Thank the Lord that His real presence speaks to us reassuring us of our relationship with Him. Thank the Lord that he delights to reassure us of His presence and relationship with us.

Ask the Lord to give you ears to hear His voice in your spirit.

5 - THE TESTIMONY OF HIS WORD

We have seen over the last couple of chapters that our assurance of salvation comes from the presence of the Lord Jesus in our lives and His testimony to our spirits. In this chapter we will look at another important means of assurance.

God has given us His Word in written form. God does not change, nor does His Word. Jesus reassured us of this in Matthew 5:18 when He said:

> *Until heaven and earth disappear, not the smallest letter, not the least stroke of a pen, will by any means disappear from the Law until everything is accomplished.*

We can count on the Word of God. It is absolutely trustworthy.

There are some very powerful statements found in the pages of the Word of God. John 3.18 tells us plainly:

Whoever believes in him is not condemned, but whoever does not believe stands condemned already because he has not believed in the name of God's one and only Son.

We have already seen that it is possible for an individual to believe things about Jesus and not be saved from the penalty of sin. John 3:18 is not speaking about a belief that Jesus exists or in why He came, although this is an important part of the meaning of the word "believe." The Greek word used here carries with it the sense of entrusting our eternal spiritual destiny into Jesus' hands. The person who truly believes is one who invests everything he or she has in Christ and His work.

In the book of Genesis we read the story of how Joseph was sold into slavery and became the manager of Potiphar's household. We are told in Genesis 39:4 that Potiphar entrusted Joseph with everything he had. Notice how this worked itself out in Potiphar's life according to Genesis 39:6:

So he left in Joseph's care everything he had; with Joseph in charge, he did not concern himself with anything except the food he ate.

For Potiphar, believing in Joseph meant that he did not concern himself with anything. He placed his full confidence in Joseph. This is the type of belief John speaks about here. If we say we believe in Jesus for our salvation, we will, like Potiphar, leave this matter entirely in His hands. We will commit the matter completely to Him.

When we can truly say that we believe in this way, and our entire confidence is in Christ we have His promise in John 3:18 that we will not be condemned. We will not be condemned because it is Christ who pays for us and keeps us. It is His work that guarantees our salvation. If it were up to me, I would never have assurance, because I will always fail. My belief is not in myself, however, but in an all-powerful and loving Christ. I trust Him and His promise that says clear: "Whoever believes in Him is not condemned" (John 3:18). In this there is great assurance.

There is another promise in Hebrews 13:5:

> God has said, "Never will I leave you; never will I forsake you."

What a wonderful promise this is. We have seen that our hope of salvation is in the presence of Christ in us. He promises those in whom He lives that he will never leave. I will not get to the end of my spiritual journey and discover that Christ abandoned me on the way. His presence will remain in me continually assuring me of my home in heaven.

I do not always deserve that He would remain with me. I can grieve His Spirit at times and even fall into sin. The promise of God remains, however: "NEVER will I leave you, NEVER will I forsake you." When I made my wedding vows to my wife, I promised that I would love and honor her in sickness and in health, for better or for worse. This is the promise God is making here in this passage. He is telling us that He will remain in us. Even in the bad times when I have failed Him God will remain faithful to me. His commitment to me is stronger than any commitment I could make to my wife. When He comes to live in our heart, He comes to stay, for better or for worse.

1 John 5:18 reassures us that Christ will also keep us safe from the evil one:

> *We know that anyone born of God does not continue to sin; the one who was born of God keeps him safe, and the evil one cannot harm him.*

Satan is more powerful than I am but the Lord God is with me. This means that I am guarded and protected against my worst enemy. Satan, though he tries with all His might, cannot separate me from the care of my heavenly Father who promises to keep me. This does not mean that I will never suffer for my faith. Satan will often buffet me but he will never be able to overcome and strip me of my relationship with God. Scripture promises that God will keep us safe from our greatest spiritual enemy.

With Christ in us we have power to overcome any temptation, trial or enemy that rises up against us. The apostle John tells us in 1 John 4:4:

You, dear children, are from God and have overcome them, because the one who is in you is greater than the one who is in the world.

Is there anything big enough or strong enough to take you from the Lord? He is bigger than any sin you will fall into. He is bigger than any spiritual or physical obstacle you will ever face. He is bigger than Satan and all his angels. If Christ is in you and He has promised never to leave you then your destiny is in the hands of a God who can never fail. Surrender to Him and trust Him to keep you.

The apostle Paul, writing to the Romans in Romans 8:35-39 told them this:

Who shall separate us from the love of Christ? Shall trouble or hardship or persecution or famine or nakedness or danger or sword? As it is written: "For your sake we face death all day long; we are considered as sheep to be slaughtered." No, in all these things we are more than conquerors through him who loved us. For I am convinced that neither death nor life, neither angels nor demons, neither the present nor the future, nor any powers, neither height nor depth, nor anything else in all creation, will be able to separate us from the love of God that is in Christ Jesus our Lord.

Scripture makes is quite clear that there is no force in heaven, hell or this earth that can ever separate us from the love of the Lord Jesus.

Notice what Paul says in this passage. He tells us that nothing can separate us from the love of Christ. It is important that we understand that we are speaking here about the love of Christ for us and not our love for Christ. Our love for Christ often fails. We do not always love Him as we should. Throughout the Scriptures the Lord speaks to His children about their failing love. While my love for Christ will often fail, Paul tells us here that Christ's love for me is very different. Nothing in all of creation is big enough break *Christ's love* for me. My assurance can never be in how much I love Christ but rather in how much Christ loves me. My love fluctuates but His will always be strong and stable. Nothing will change His love for me. This is my confidence.

We have yet another promise from the God who cannot lie recorded for us in Philippians 1.6:

Being confident of this, that he who began a good

work in you will carry it on to completion until the day of Christ Jesus.

What the Lord Jesus has begun in your life, He will complete. He has committed Himself to us and is devoted to completing what He has begun in our lives. Notice that it is Christ who began the work in us and it is Christ who will carry in on to completion. This verse is not about me and my efforts; it is about Christ and what He is doing in me.

He will continue the work He began in us until we meet Him face to face. Jude 1:24 puts it this way:

To him who is able to keep you from falling and to present you before his glorious presence without fault and with great joy- to the only God our Saviour be glory, majesty, power and authority, through Jesus Christ our Lord, before all ages, now and forever more! Amen.

What wonderful promises we have in these verses. What the Lord Jesus began in our lives He will bring to completion. Salvation is not so much a believer's commitment to the Lord Jesus as it is Christ's commitment to the believer. He came to offer His life to pay the penalty we could not pay. He comes to live in the life of those whose hearts have been opened to receive Him. He promises never to leave us. He commits Himself to keeping and protecting us. His desire is to present us before His father without fault or accusation. Salvation is the work of Christ Jesus in our lives accepting, forgiving, keeping and shaping us into the image of His Father.

What is important for us to note here is that the Lord Jesus has made a commitment to us. We have the promise of His Word that He will who begun a work in us will continue and complete that work. His love for us will never change, though ours may be fleeting and shallow at times. He promises to keep us safe and present us before the Father one day without fault. This is His promise to us. Our assurance of salvation comes from "Christ in us", the testimony of His Spirit, and the word of a God who cannot lie.

For Consideration:

What are the promises of Christ to the believer in this chapter?

Could we ever have assurance of salvation if that assurance depended on me?

How does knowing that you assurance of salvation rests fully in Christ and His work give you confidence? Will the Lord fail in His promises? Is He able to overcome the obstacles you face in life and present you to the Father?

For Prayer:

Thank the Lord that while we are often weak and fail that He is faithful to His commitment to us.

Ask the Lord to forgive you for the times you looked to yourself for the assurance of salvation. Thank Him that your salvation is not guaranteed on the basis of your efforts but in the perfect work he has done.

Thank the Lord for the promises of Scripture that assure us of His commitment to us.

6 - CONCLUDING WORDS

If there is one thing I would like each reader to take from this brief study of the assurance of salvation, it is that any assurance we have must be based on the work of Christ. I will never have any full assurance of salvation if I am looking to myself or my efforts for this assurance.

The reality is that I will always fail. My love for Christ will not always be what it should be. I will not always live the life I ought to live. At best I am unworthy of the salvation the Lord offers. If I look to myself, I will always have cause for concern.

My assurance rest in three things—the presence of Christ in me, the reassuring testimony of His Spirit to my spirit, and the promises of His Word. Christ alone is my assurance. There is no assurance apart from Him. I am reassured not because of what *I* do but because of

Christ's work in me. I am reassured not because I feel *I* have a strong commitment to Christ but because *He* has committed Himself to me.

Do you know the salvation of the Lord Jesus today? I'm not asking you if you are a religious person. I am not even asking you if you believe a certain set of doctrines. My concern is not primarily about the kind of life you are living. My concern is whether you have opened your heart to the forgiveness and work of the Lord Jesus and His Spirit. Salvation is more about what Jesus is doing than about what we are doing. Have you experienced His cleansing and renewing work? Has the indwelling Spirit given you assurance that you belong to Christ?

If you do not have this assurance today, I invite you to turn your attention to the only One who can give you that assurance. Ask Him to forgive you. Ask Him to come into your life to work out His salvation in you. Stop trusting in what you have been doing and put your complete and undivided confidence in what Jesus has done and will do in you.

True assurance of salvation can only come as we place our complete and total confidence and trust in the presence of the Lord Jesus and His work, the convicting testimony of His Spirit in us and the unfailing Word of His promise as found in the pages Scripture.

ABOUT THE AUTHOR

Light To My Path Book Distribution

Light To My Path Book Distribution (LTMP) is a book writing and distribution ministry reaching out to needy Christian workers in Asia, Latin America, and Africa. Many Christian workers in developing countries do not have the resources necessary to obtain Bible training or  purchase Bible study materials for their ministries and personal encouragement.

F. Wayne Mac Leod is a member of Action International Ministries and has been writing these books with a goal to distribute them freely or at cost price to needy pastors and Christian workers around the world. To date thousands of are being used in preaching, teaching, evangelism and encouragement of local believers in over sixty countries. Books in these series have now been translated a number of languages. The goal is to make them available to as many believers as possible.

The ministry of LTMP is a faith based ministry and we trust the Lord for the resources necessary to distribute the books for the encouragement and strengthening of believers around the world. Would you pray that the Lord would open doors for the translation and further distribution of these books?

For more information about Light To My Path visit our website at www.lighttomypath.ca

Made in the USA
Middletown, DE
12 October 2023

40702361R00035